KWANZAA

Written and Compiled by
Rod Terry

Illustrations by
Angela Williams, Ashante Studios

THE SEVEN PRINCIPLES

PETER PAUPER PRESS, INC.
WHITE PLAINS, NEW YORK

For my loving and devoted friend, Juanita Dean, Esq.

Text copyright © 1996
Peter Pauper Press, Inc.
202 Mamaroneck Avenue
White Plains, NY 10601
Illustrations copyright © 1992, 1996
Angela Williams, Ashante Studios
All rights reserved
ISBN 0-88088-355-3
Printed in Singapore
7 6 5 4 3 2 1

Contents

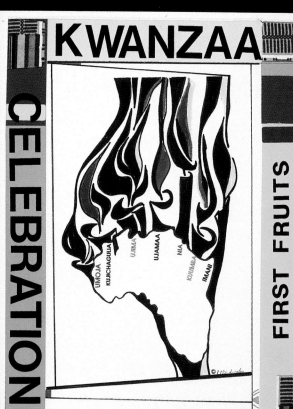

KWANZAA

CELEBRATION

FIRST FRUITS

KWANZAA

UMOJA
KUJICHAGULIA
UJIMA
UJAMAA
NIA
KUUMBA
IMANI

INTRODUCTION

Kwanzaa is a spiritual celebration that is observed each year from December 26th through January 1st. The word Kwanzaa is derived from a Kiswahili phrase, *matunda ya kwanza*, which means the "first fruits of the harvest." Kwanzaa was first celebrated in 1966 by Dr. Maulana Karenga, a Black Studies professor and black activist. America's fastest-growing holiday, Kwanzaa is observed by an estimated 18 million people.

The celebration of Kwanzaa is a means for African-Americans to reaffirm their commitment to themselves, their families, their community, and the black struggle. Dr. Karenga envisioned that Kwanzaa would provide African-Americans with spiritual renewal and sustenance, as well as an opportunity for us to connect with our rich cultural heritage.

Kwanzaa is based on seven principles: *Umoja* (unity), *Kujichagulia* (self-determination), *Ujima* (collective work and responsibility), *Ujamaa* (cooperative economics), *Nia* (purpose), *Kuumba* (creativity), and *Imani* (faith). These seven principles are collectively referred to as the *Nguzo Saba*, and are intended to serve as guideposts for meditation and daily living.

Kwanzaa also incorporates seven symbols from African culture that have significant ritualistic meaning. The seven symbols are *mazao* (fruits, vegetables, and nuts), *mkeka* (place mat), *kinara* (candleholder), *vibunzi* or *muhindi* (ears of corn), *zawadi* (gifts), *kikombe cha umoja* (communal cup of unity), and *mishumaa saba* (seven candles).

Each night of the celebration a different candle is lit to represent the principle for that day, and celebrants engage in discussions about the meaning of the principle. Generally, stories and folk tales are told to illustrate the importance of each tenet.

Kwanzaa: The Seven Principles explores the meaning and significance of each principle of Kwanzaa, suggests how the principles can be applied to everyday life, and includes inspirational thoughts and quotations by notable African-Americans relative to the philosophy of each principle. This book is intended to be used throughout the year as a source of inspiration and a guide for spiritual well-being, as well as a companion for celebrating Kwanzaa.

R. T.

PRONUNCIATION KEY

The Seven Principles:

Umoja (Oo-moe-ja)

Kujichagulia (Koo-ji-cha-goo-lia)

Ujima (Oo-ji-ma)

Ujamaa (Oo-ja-ma)

Nia (Nee-ah)

Kuumba (Koo-um-ba)

Imani (I-ma-ni)

The Seven Symbols:

Mazao (Mah-zah-oh)

Mkeka (M-kay-kah)

Kinara (Kee-nah-rah)

Vibunzi (Vee-boon-zee); Muhindi (Moo-heen-dee)

Zawadi (Sah-wah-dee)

Kikombe Cha Umoja (Kee-coam-bay Chah Oo-moe-ja)

Mishumaa Saba (Mee-shoo-ma-ah Sah-bah)

UMOJA

UNITY

©1992 ALW

To strive for
and maintain
unity in the family. . .

UNITY

UMOJA

UMOJA
Unity

Umoja is the first principle of Kwanzaa. It is symbolized by lighting the black candle in the center of the *kinara*, which represents unity. Unity is appropriately celebrated the first day of Kwanzaa because it is the common thread that ties us all together. Our progress as a race depends on our ability to form cohesive bonds that transcend our individual differences.

Umoja encourages us to strive for and to maintain unity in the family, community, race, and nation. Throughout history, great black thinkers have always advocated the benefits of a unified race. As early as 1847, Frederick Douglass declared, "Our cause is one, and we must help each other, if we would succeed." *Umoja* helps us to understand that in order for African-Americans to live more peaceful and fruitful lives we must strengthen and build our families and communities into a unified force that works for the common good.

The familiar proverb, "When spider webs unite–they can tie up a lion," is a testament to the strength of a unified force. The proverb clearly illuminates *Umoja*'s example that we are stronger and more effective in our communities and in the nation as a whole when we unite and form strong familial and cultural ties.

One God! One Aim! One Destiny!

MARCUS GARVEY

Injustice anywhere is a threat to justice everywhere. We are caught in an inescapable network of mutuality, tied in a single garment of destiny. Whatever affects one directly affects all indirectly.

MARTIN LUTHER KING, JR.

We are one people and must strive to act as
one. As a people, our realities, life chances
and possibilities are rooted in the quality of
our relations with each other.

DR. MAULANA KARENGA

Blacks must recapture the sense of a national
black community that they had before the
1960s civil rights protest period. Black cooperation and unity are essential tools for building empowerment . . .

CLAUD ANDERSON

We have to give up the narrow individualistic
approach so that the brother in Harlem can
relate to the brothers in Mississippi and feel
that common bond. I believe the best chance
for black survival lies in black solidarity, with
the mental strength to deal in the affairs of
the whole world.

DR. ALVIN POUSSAINT

Afro-Americans must unite and work together. We must take pride in the Afro-American
community, for it is our home and it is our
power.

MALCOLM X

We make our living by what we get. We
make our life by what we give.

BENJAMIN E. MAYS

It is the family that gives us a deep private
sense of belonging. Here we first begin to
have our self defined for us.

HOWARD THURMAN

I would not know how to be a human being
at all, except I learned this from other human
beings. We are made for a delicate network of
relationships, of interdependence. Not even
the most powerful nation can be completely
self-sufficient.

BISHOP DESMOND TUTU

The woman came charging toward me, her bare feet slapping the earth, and snatching her baby free, she thrust it at me almost roughly, the gesture saying "Take it!" . . . and I did, clasping the baby to me. Then she snatched away her baby; and another woman was thrusting her baby, then another, and another . . . I wouldn't learn until maybe a year later [that I was] participating in one of the oldest ceremonies of humankind, called "The laying on of hands."

ALEX HALEY,
Roots

What unites us is far greater than what divides us as families and friends and Americans and spiritual sojourners on this Earth.

MARIAN WRIGHT EDELMAN

The ultimate destiny and aspiration of the African people and twenty million American Negroes are magnificently bound up together forever.

LORRAINE HANSBERRY

There is no separate freedom or dignity for African men and women.

DR. MAULANA KARENGA

We are close to the last chance we have to solve the problematic nature of the relationship between white and black. It is a relationship we have inherited. It is a heritage that is unworthy of our children and grandchildren. We have been dragging our problems of history around with us like a sack of cotton.

AUGUST WILSON

Blacks and whites must meet and know each other as brothers in a marriage of visions, as co-conspirators in the making of a dream, as fellow passengers on a journey into the unknown.

LERONE BENNETT, JR.

The idea of separation is harkening to the past and it is undesirable even if it could be realized, because the progress of mankind has been based upon contact and association, upon social, intellectual and cultural contact.

A. PHILIP RANDOLPH

SELF–DETERMINATION

kujichagulia

KUJICHAGULIA

To define ourselves,

CREATE FOR OURSELVES,

. . .SPEAK for OURSELVES. . .

© 1992 AW

Self Determination

KUJICHAGULIA
Self-Determination

The second principle of Kwanzaa is *Kujichagulia*, which is symbolized by lighting the first red candle of the *kinara*. The significance of *Kujichagulia* is that it encourages us to define, name, create, and speak for ourselves instead of being defined, named, created for, and spoken for by others. Self-determination shapes our belief that we are responsible for our destiny in life and helps us to understand that we are our greatest resource. As history has taught, we cannot expect from others what we must provide for ourselves. *Kujichagulia* instills in us a sense of independence and self-sufficiency.

The Million Man March on Washington embodies the essence of the lessons espoused by *Kujichagulia*. The March was a clarion call for African-American men to take control of their destinies, and in an unprecedented show of solidarity and unity, a vast multitude of black men vowed to take renewed responsibility for themselves, their families, and their communities.

To achieve any measure of the type of self-discovery inspired by Kujichagulia, we must have a clear and thorough understanding of our history. Despite our distance from Africa, our motherland, we cannot ignore her values and traditions. "Just as the Sankofa bird must revisit its history to determine its destiny, a people must know from whence they came to know whence they are going." Once we understand our history we are able to shape our future.

You are unique—there is no one else like you.
MARVA COLLINS

You have to know that your real home is within.
QUINCY JONES

You can't be nobody but who you are . . .
that shadow wasn't nothing but you growing
into yourself. You either got to grow into it or
cut it down to fit you. But that's all you got
to make life with. That's all you got to measure yourself against that world out there.

AUGUST WILSON

We have been named; we should now
become "namers."

LERONE BENNETT, JR.

He belongs someplace. The day he was given
a name he was also given a place which no
one but he himself can fill.

MAYA ANGELOU

If I didn't define myself for myself, I would be
crunched into other people's fantasies for me
and eaten alive.

AUDRE LORDE

Put your brains to thinking for self; your feet
to walking in the direction of self; your hands
to working for self and your children.

ELIJAH MUHAMMAD

To acknowledge our ancestors means we are
aware that we did not make ourselves, that
the line stretches all the way back, perhaps to
God, or to Gods. We remember them
because it is an easy thing to forget; that we
are not the first to suffer, rebel, fight, love,
and die. The grace with which we embrace
life, in spite of the pain, the sorrows, is always
a measure of what has gone before.

ALICE WALKER

There is nothing more correct for African
Americans than to search for and follow our
own historical traditions.

MOLEFI KETE ASANTE

We can't rely on anyone but ourselves to
define our existence, to shape the image of
ourselves.

SPIKE LEE

Acceptance of prevailing standards often
means we have no standards of our own.

JEAN TOOMER

One of the first things I think young people, especially nowadays, should learn is how to see for yourself and listen for yourself and think for yourself. Then you can come to an intelligent decision for yourself.

MALCOLM X

The first act of a self-conscious, self-determining people . . . is to redefine and reshape reality in its own image and according to its own needs.

DR. MAULANA KARENGA

A race of people is like an individual man; until it uses its own talent, takes pride in its own history, expresses its own culture, affirms its own selfhood, it can never fulfill itself.

MALCOLM X

As a people, we must remember that we are not as weak as we have allowed ourselves to be painted and we are not as strong as we *can* be.

JOHN E. JACOB

No one else can retrieve our values and salvage our people better than we can.

DOROTHY I. HEIGHT

When I took the big leap, when I left Motown and went out on my own, all I really wanted is the same thing I want now: to be in charge of myself and my life.

DIANA ROSS

If my life has had any meaning at all, it is that those who start out as outcasts can wind up as being part of the system. Maybe others can forget what it was like to be excluded from the dining rooms in this very building, Senator, but I shall not forget.

PATRICIA ROBERTS HARRIS,
At her confirmation hearing as Secretary of HUD

We are survivors, not victims, and we have to take a stand . . . that allows us to move from being the victim of other people's decisions to the architect of our own well-being.

LANI GUINIER

It is time for Blacks to take charge of their fate and to refuse to permit White liberals and Black sycophants to continue leading the race down a primrose path to ultimate oblivion.

JOE CLARK

Can't nothing make your life work if you ain't the architect.

TERRY MCMILLAN

The most worthwhile endeavor I have ever undertaken is responsibility for my own life. It's hard, and it's worth it.

LEVAR BURTON

I believe in the soul. Furthermore, I believe it is prompt accountability for one's choices, a willing acceptance of responsibility for one's thoughts, behavior, and actions that makes it powerful.

ALICE WALKER

A dream doesn't become reality through magic; it takes sweat, determination and hard work.

COLIN L. POWELL

Nothing ever comes to one, that is worth having, except as a result of hard work.

BOOKER T. WASHINGTON

We get closer to God as we get more intimately and understandingly acquainted with the things He has created. I know of nothing more inspiring than that of making discoveries for one's self.

GEORGE WASHINGTON CARVER

If we do not dare everything, the fulfillment of that prophecy, re-created from the Bible in song by a slave, is upon us: *God gave Noah the rainbow sign, No more water, the fire next time!*

JAMES BALDWIN,
The Fire Next Time

UJIMA ••

TO BUILD AND MAINTAIN OUR

© 1992 Assir

Community Together

Our Brothers' and Sisters' problems

our problems

COLLECTIVE WORK

AND RESPONSIBILITY

UJIMA ••

UJIMA
Collective Work and Responsibility

Ujima, the third principle of Kwanzaa, is symbolized by lighting the first green candle of the *kinara*. *Ujima* is based on the notion that African-Americans must work together to build and maintain our communities, and that we must make our sisters' and brothers' problems our very own and solve them together. *Ujima* is a call for cooperation, accountability, and compassion.

The first step to effect positive change within our community is to engender a spirit of cooperation. Cooperation requires us to work together for the common good. A spirit of cooperation sets the stage for us to build joint partnerships focusing on measures that promote our community's interests and provide for our needs. As a second step, we must be willing to take full responsibility for ourselves, our families, the community, and the future.

Finally, we must treat each other with compassion and respect. The idea that we have

an obligation to be concerned about the problems and welfare of each other is what Dr. Martin Luther King Jr. referred to as the "breath of life." According to Dr. King, "An individual has not started living until he can rise above the narrow confines of his individualistic concerns to the broader concerns of all humanity."

Any black who strives to achieve in this country should think in terms of not only himself, but also how he can reach down and grab another black child and pull him to the top of the mountain where he is. This is what a gold medal does to you.

JESSE OWENS

History reminds us that our life traditions were wholly encompassed by our kinships and tribes. No children and mothers were ever unsheltered and unprotected.

DOROTHY I. HEIGHT

Black power is black responsibility.
ADAM CLAYTON POWELL, JR.

Black Americans must begin to accept a larger share of responsibility for their lives. . . . To fight any battle takes soldiers who are strong, healthy, committed, well-trained, and confident.
JESSE L. JACKSON, JR.

Those of us who, by the grace of God, have escaped the legacy of racism and poverty and now enjoy a comfortable life have an obligation to help where we can.
ARMSTRONG WILLIAMS

Breaking barriers! Just as no man is an island in the sea of human hopes and hatreds, so no man is capable of bashing alone the roadblocks to justice and human freedom.
CARL ROWAN

Our future lies in the philosophy of love and understanding and caring and building, not of hatred and tearing down.
COLIN L. POWELL

We realize that our future lies chilly in our
hands. We know that neither institutions nor
friends can make a race stand unless it has
strength in its own foundation; that races like
individuals must stand or fall by their own
merit; that to fully succeed they must prac-
tice the virtues of self reliance, self respect,
industry, perseverance, and economy.

PAUL ROBESON

Like every man, every woman must decide
whether she will walk in the light of creative
altruism or the darkness of destructive selfish-
ness. This is the judgment. Life's most persis-
tent and urgent question is, what are you
doing for others?

MARTIN LUTHER KING, JR.

I learned that no matter what you may or
may not have, as perceived by a misguided
community about what is valuable, people
understand hard work and talent–and it can
prevail.

MAXINE WATERS

If you and I don't build a bridge back, throw out some strong lifelines to our children, youth and families whom poverty, unemployment are engulfing, they're going to drown, pull many of us down with them and undermine the future our forebears dreamed, struggled, and died for.

MARIAN WRIGHT EDELMAN

Our road to that glorious future lies through collective hard work to accomplish the objectives of creating a people centered society.

NELSON MANDELA

Wake up. The hour has come to be more responsible. Change this world by starting with yourself. The world is not going to change until you change.

DR. BETTY SHABAZZ

Chance has never yet satisfied the hope of a suffering people. Action, self-reliance, the vision of self and the future have been the only means by which the oppressed have seen and realized the light of their own freedom.

MARCUS GARVEY

UJAMAA

ECONOMICS

COOPERATIVE

To maintain our own stores. . .

shops. . . businesses. . .

ujamaa

UJAMAA
Cooperative Economics

On the fourth day of Kwanzaa, *Ujamaa*, the second red candle is lit on the *kinara*. *Ujamaa* stresses the benefits and advantages of practicing cooperative economics in African-American communities. *Ujamaa* is based on the concept that African-Americans must strive to build, maintain, and support their own businesses. *Ujamaa* helps us to understand and appreciate that black empowerment can be accomplished only through group economics and a cooperative work ethic.

Our prosperity depends on our ability to merge our social, financial, and political resources to achieve common goals and shared benefits. Our economic resources should be kept and circulated within our community, so they can be reinvested in our schools, businesses, and churches.

A new school of thought has recently emerged suggesting that leadership in the

African-American community should be institutional rather than centered around charismatic personalities. There is a direct correlation between cooperative economics and institution-building. To build viable, influential, and strong institutions and businesses that protect and defend our interests, we must unite as a race and pool our economic resources. Our influence in the United States and throughout the world depends on our ability to achieve economic empowerment.

To achieve self-sufficiency, blacks must master the principles of capitalism and group economics.

CLAUD ANDERSON

At the bottom of education, at the bottom of politics, even at the bottom of religion, there must be economic independence.

BOOKER T. WASHINGTON

When we are noted for enterprise, industry, and success, we shall no longer have any trouble in the matter of civil and political rights.

FREDERICK DOUGLASS

Economic self-sufficiency is the foundation upon which society is built. The value of a family to a society is that it makes the capital investment in the individual members . . .

TONY BROWN

Without money, you have no control. Without control, you have no power.

SPIKE LEE

The core of the civil rights problem is the matter of achieving equal opportunity for Negroes in the labor market. For it stands to reason that all our other civil rights depend on that one for fulfillment. We cannot afford better education for our children, better housing or medical care unless we have jobs.

WHITNEY M. YOUNG, JR.

A man's bread and butter is only insured
when he works for it.

MARCUS GARVEY

We need to run our own businesses more, and
we need to run them the way Du Bois ran
Niagara, the way Healy ran Georgetown, the
way Johnson ran *Jet*, the way Gaston ran part
of Birmingham, the way Gordy ran Motown,
the way Reggie Lewis ran Beatrice.

RALPH WILEY

Keeping dollars in the black community cre-
ates new jobs, makes services more accessible
to the poor and the elderly, and contributes to
a sense of community pride.

EDWARD W. BROOKE

To be a poor man is hard, but to be a poor
race in a land of dollars is the very bottom of
hardships.

W. E. B. DU BOIS

Money is no good unless it contributes something to the community, unless it builds a bridge to a better life. Any man can make money, but it takes a special kind of man to use it responsibly.

A. G. GASTON

Money has no color. If you can build a better mousetrap, it won't matter whether you're black or white, people will buy it.

A. G. GASTON

My object in life is not simply to make money for myself or to spend it on myself. I love to use a part of what I make in trying to help others.

MADAM C. J. WALKER

If we want to see ourselves in a positive manner, then we must learn to register our votes with our dollars.

CICELY TYSON

We have to be accountable for the state of our race. Our bondage and our battle is economic. We're not slaves but servants. We have to spend more time at economic conferences, be producers and provide jobs. The answer is economic self-sufficiency.

SHIRLEY CHISHOLM

Where big money stays, big decisions are made.

JESSE L. JACKSON, JR.

I always tried to raise money for the Black Panthers through business schemes. To develop political and economic power in a capitalist society, you need capital.

BOBBY SEALE

To survive in the rapidly approaching pluralistic society, blacks must create a black economy. To develop economically, black dollars must bounce or exchange hands eight-to-10 times before leaving the black community.

CLAUD ANDERSON

PURPOSE

NIA

NIA
Purpose

Nia, the fifth principle of Kwanzaa, is symbolized by lighting the second green candle of
the *kinara*. *Nia* charges that we must develop
ourselves and then work collectively to build
and develop our communities, so that we can
restore our people to their traditional
greatness.

Each of us is born into life with a divine
purpose. The principle of *Nia* encourages us
to get in touch with our inner being. Once
we determine who we are and understand
the nature of our existence, we will be able
to reach our fullest potential in life. Self-
realization focuses our energy and frees us
of insecurities and doubts, which allows us to
concentrate our efforts on the *Nguzo Saba*.

I recall attending my sister's graduation cere-
mony at Spelman College in Atlanta,
Georgia, at which Oprah Winfrey delivered
the commencement address. She confided to
the graduates that she had squandered her

twenties; it was not until she reached her thirties and became more centered and focused that she was able to build her multi-million-dollar entertainment enterprise. Oprah Winfrey's life is a perfect illustration of the type of action and self-fulfillment *Nia* encourages.

The most valuable lesson instilled by *Nia* is that we all have the power to make a difference to ourselves and in our communities. Each of us is a unique and divine original, created on-purpose, with a purpose. We didn't just happen.

SUSAN L. TAYLOR

It's pretty hard for the Lord to guide you if you haven't made up your mind which way you want to go.

MADAM C. J. WALKER

I am not sure who I am, but I have given all of me that I can find to the pursuit of this consuming purpose, and the answer to the question is beginning to make itself known even to me.

HOWARD THURMAN

Every man has a place in this world, but no man has to designate that place.

PEARL BAILEY

Defining myself, as opposed to being defined by others, is one of the most difficult challenges I face.

CAROL MOSELEY BRAUN

Always continue the climb. It is possible for you to do whatever you choose, if you first get to know who you are and are willing to work with a power that is greater than ourselves to do it.

OPRAH WINFREY

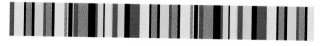

Each generation must, out of relative obscurity, discover its mission, fulfill it, or betray it.

FRANTZ FANON

We create our own destiny by the way we do things. We have to take advantage of opportunities and be responsible for our choices.

BENJAMIN CARSON

There is a great wisdom in the message of self-reliance, education, of hard work, and of the need to raise strong families.

COLIN L. POWELL

I will not allow one prejudiced person or one million or one hundred million to blight my life. I will not let prejudice or any of its attendant humiliations and injustices bear me down to spiritual defeat. My inner life is mine, and I shall defend and maintain its integrity against all the powers of hell.

JAMES WELDON JOHNSON

It must be borne in mind that the tragedy of life doesn't lie in not reaching your goal. The tragedy lies in having no goal to reach. It isn't a calamity to die with dreams unfulfilled, but it is a calamity not to dream. It is not a disaster to be unable to capture your ideal, but it is a disaster to have no ideal to capture. It is not a disgrace not to reach the stars, but it is a disgrace to have no stars to reach for. Not failure, but low aim, is sin.

BENJAMIN E. MAYS

People ought to do what they want to do, what else are they alive for?

JAMES BALDWIN

At the core of life is a hard purposefulness, a *determination* to live.

HOWARD THURMAN

I promoted myself. I had to make my own living and my own opportunity! But I made it! Don't sit down and wait for the opportunities to come. Get up and make them!

MADAM C. J. WALKER

Our flag is red, white and blue, but our nation is a rainbow—red, yellow, brown, black and white—and we're all precious in God's sight. . . . Even in our fractured state, all of us count and all of us fit somewhere.

JESSE L. JACKSON, JR.

Mama exhorted her children at every opportunity to "jump at de sun." We might not land on the sun, but at least we would get off the ground.

ZORA NEALE HURSTON

To be Black is to shine and aim high.

LEONTYNE PRICE

I'll tell you something, honey: I would have made a very good president. That's right! *Me!* I would have done well. I'm honest and I'm tough and I could get the job done, yes, sir!

BESSIE DELANY,
Having Our Say

KUUMBA

CREATIVITY

CREATIVITY

kuumba

KUUMBA
Creativity

Kuumba is the sixth principle of Kwanzaa. It is symbolized by lighting the last red candle of the *kinara*.

Kuumba challenges us always to do as much as we possibly can, in the best way we can, in order to better our community. *Kuumba* encourages us to use our creative skills, talents, and imagination to build long-lasting and strong institutions that become our vanguards, especially in the fight for equal justice. It is the creative mind that is able to shape and forge solutions that lead to progress.

Growing up in the South in the 1970s, I remember always being told to work and study hard so I would grow up to be "a credit to the race." Those words inspired in me an almost obsessive need to excel. The idea of being "a credit to the race" was a mantra that reverberated throughout the black community. It set the standard for achievement, and for many it was a basis for motivation and

creativity. In a sense, this is the same lesson espoused by *Kuumba.*

Dr. Martin Luther King, Jr., once declared that "potential powers of creativity are within each of us, and we have a duty to work assiduously to discover these powers."

The Egyptian pyramids are an astonishing example of the creative genius of our people. Our ancestors left behind the pyramids so that we would constantly be reminded of the greatness of our African heritage and our ability to dream and create the magnificent. It is our obligation to use our God-given talents, skills, and abilities so that we might become "a credit to the race."

Invest in the human soul. Who knows, it might be a diamond in the rough.
MARY MCLEOD BETHUNE

Creativity is something that can happen only in the mind. It doesn't matter whether you're dealing with clay or paints or words or just your way of living. . . . we are the most creative people in the world, which is an extraordinary thing.

BILL GUNN

Life is pure adventure, and the sooner we realize that, the quicker we will be able to treat life as art: to bring all our energies to each encounter, to remain flexible enough to notice and admit when what we expected to happen did not happen. We need to remember that we are created creative and can invent new scenarios as frequently as they are needed.

MAYA ANGELOU

Yeah, life hurts like hell, but this is how I keep going. I have a sense of humor. I've got my brothers and sisters. I've got this ability to make something out of nothing. I can clap my hands and make magic.

BILL T. JONES

The principle of *Kuumba* instills in us the value for creative labor which will not only increase our capacity to liberate ourselves, but also make the profound and far-reaching contribution to human history of which we as a people are capable.

DR. MAULANA KARENGA

Every people should be the originators of their own designs, the projectors of their own schemes, and creators of the events that lead to their destiny—the consummation of their own desires.

MARTIN DELANY

We are creative beings, and God is always offering us creative ideas that we can act upon to liberate and fulfill ourselves.

SUSAN L. TAYLOR

When you look in the mirror, know who is looking back at you. When you know your strengths and recognize your weaknesses, you can create art.

DEBBIE ALLEN

For four hundred years African creativity
has been struggling to counter the narrow
constraints of oppression, to circle it, turn it
around, to seek order and meaning in the
midst of chaos. My soul looks back in wonder
at how African creativity has sustained us and
how it still flows–seeking, searching for new
ways to connect the ancient with the new,
the young with the old, the unborn with the
ancestors.

TOM FEELINGS

I've always had confidence. It came because
I have lots of initiative. I wanted to make
something of myself.

EDDIE MURPHY

The human spirit cannot be tamed and
should not be trained.

NIKKI GIOVANNI

I think once you stop wanting to create,
wanting to work and push forward, you
become old. And then you die.

DIANA ROSS

IMANI

TO BELIEVE IN OUR SELVES

OUR PARENTS,

OUR GOD. . . .

FAITH

FAITH

IMANI

IMANI
Faith

The last principle of Kwanzaa is *Imani. Imani,* which is symbolized by lighting the last green candle of the *kinara,* teaches us to have un-yielding faith in our Creator and our people.

Life is unpredictable. Our circumstances change from day to day. One moment we are on top of the world enjoying the bounty of success; the next moment we must deal with the anguish of defeat. As expressed by the poet Maya Angelou, "There are many inci-dents which can eviscerate the stalwart and bring the mighty down." In order to survive in this ever-changing environment, we must be guided and strengthened by faith. Faith gives us anchorage in the storms of life.

Imani emphasizes belief in our Creator, race, parents, teachers, and leaders, in addition to the righteousness of our struggle. Belief in our families and our race fosters a strong sense of security and gives us unflappable courage. With unwavering faith in ourselves,

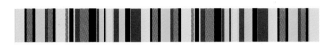

the support of our families, and trust in God, there is no obstacle we cannot overcome.

It is this belief in a power larger than myself and other than myself which allows me to venture into the unknown and even the unknowable.

MAYA ANGELOU

If Black America is to ever get on its feet, it must first get down on its knees.

RALPH D. ABERNATHY

Faith can live only so long as it is being used. Every time you master failure, your faith becomes stronger and you are better pre-pared to meet your next obstacle. Faith applied–put to work–is the beginning of all self-confidence, all self-reliance.

DENNIS KIMBRO AND NAPOLEON HILL

I act as if everything depends upon me and pray as if everything depends upon God.

OPRAH WINFREY

With this faith we will be able to transform the jangling discords of our nation into a beautiful symphony of brotherhood.

MARTIN LUTHER KING, JR.

In the midst of outer dangers I have felt an inner calm and known resources of strength that only God could give. In many instances I have felt the power of God transforming the fatigue of despair into the buoyancy of hope. I am convinced that the universe is under the control of a loving purpose and that in the struggle for righteousness, man has cosmic companionship.

MARTIN LUTHER KING, JR.

My relationship with God has helped me avoid problems others have run into.

BARRY SANDERS

We live by faith in others. But most of all we must live by faith in ourselves–faith to believe that we can develop into useful men and women.

BENJAMIN E. MAYS

This is the secret of life: being able to feed off the spirit.

TREMAINE HAWKINS

I am a firm believer in divine guidance. If something is going to happen, it will. Then my life will turn in a new direction. Any time I've tried to plot a plan, forget it! It never works! So I trust in where life takes me.

CICELY TYSON

Faith in God is the greatest power . . . but great, too, is faith in oneself.

MARY MCLEOD BETHUNE

Religion without humanity is a poor human stuff.

SOJOURNER TRUTH

You've got to put your faith in a higher power, live for something greater than money or houses or cars or fame. If you're living for those things, then you're going to be miserable. . . . Unless a man has his hope and his spirituality, he will die a very poor man indeed.

ARMSTRONG WILLIAMS

Once we put our trust in God when we didn't have a thing on earth. Now some of us have achievements. But we can't forget the God who brings us salvation.

EUGENE A. MARINO

I work hard to keep things around me positive. At a basic level, my belief in God lets me believe that I can achieve almost anything.

FLORENCE GRIFFITH JOYNER

At the end of the day, give up your worries and give thanks for the journey.

BEN VEREEN

BIOGRAPHICAL INDEX